Mini Guides 2016

BATHROOM DESIGNER

BRIAN RIDER

Mini Guides
2016

WHAT IS A BATH...
DESIGNER?

WHAT IS A BATHROOM DESIGNER?

Bath;room planning has more pitfalls than kitchen planning and bathroom designing is even less understood than kitchen designing. Of all the delegates on all our courses I cannot recall anyone who arrived on the course with an in depth knowledge of bathrooms and only a few who left really capable of producing a genuine designer bathroom.

We have plenty of delegates who sold bathrooms costing £20,000 plus but how many were really successful I am not sure. I am aware of only about 20 bathroom designers in the U.K

. ATTRIBUTES

* fully familiar with plumbing

* fully familiar with electrics

* fully familiar with planning aspects

* possesses a flair for design

* experienced at presentation

* fully familiar with product availability

* fully familiar with ergonomics and anthropometrics

* familiar with disabled bathroom planning

* fully conversant with wet room techniques and alternatives

FIRST EVER BATHROOM DESIGNER PUBLICATION

Can lead to a professional qualification

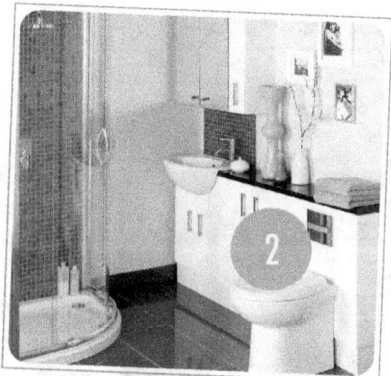

For the first time we are offering a genuine Bathroom Designer guide for professionals. Clearly you need to be fluent in all aspects of Bathroom Planning before you can begin the challenge to become a Bathroom Designer. Do any of these qualify as design?

Bath 1- 25%

Bath 2- 35%

Bath 3-15%

BATHROOM DESIGNER

Clearly this bathroom planner had no concept of design, If you really must have a washing machine in the bathroom you could at least put a door on the front to blend it in a bit. The actual effort and cost of doing that would be miniscule compared to the overall cost of the bathroom.

A bathroom designer clearly needs a bit of imagination. Why does this room have a serving hatch? A mirror would have been preferable.

BATHROOM
ERGONOMICS

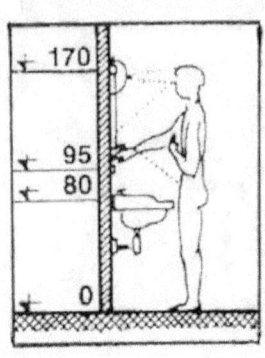 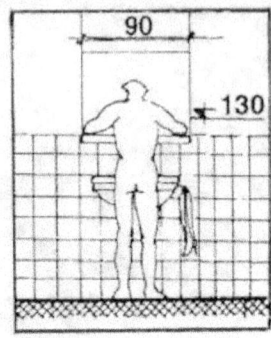 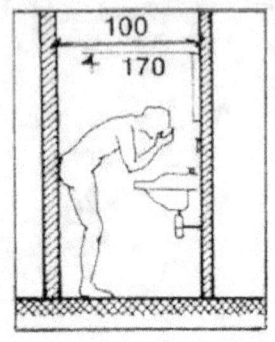

ERGONOMICS

Because the population is ageing and many older buyers have some disability to varying degrees it is extremely important to be fully familiar with the subject of ergonomics and anthropometrics both for able bodied and disabled user. No good having a German deluge shower 8 foot up on the ceiling when you are 5 foot lower in a wheel chair. Even a 25mm shower tray might be a hardship for a disabled user. And what height do you set the shower valve.?

Bathroom 1 is perfectly decorated and accessorised and is a credit to the owner and designer. If this is the main bathroom I would again question the lack of a bath, especially in this generously sized room. You will find it difficult to sell a property unless the master bathroom has a bath. If you can find the space for a bath AND a shower, so much the better.

Bathroom 2 is yet another example with a washing machine, in this case also a tumble dryer. I can appreciate that some people will want this arrangement but surely it would be child's play to make the machines less obvious. In this instance the introduction of furniture doors to cover the appliances and probably best in a double door arrangement would really have been very simple and vastly more attractive.

Bathroom 3 This is another phenomenon which seems to be creeping into American bathroom planning:- siting the bath in a wet room situation where the bath almost certainly gets drenched when you have a shower.

On one level it may have some merit in that many people would like to have a soak in the bathtub first and then go straight to the shower to get thoroughly clean.

This bathroom appears to be very much customer led. The customer obviously wanted a traditional look and a separate shower plus a freestanding bath. The planner managed to squeeze it all in, even including a bidet but it looks incredibly busy. I would question the choice of mirrors as these are not quite in keeping with the trad look. Judging by the space to the left hand of the main door it would appear that there would have been enough room for the shower, possibly an offset quad, allowing the bath a much better aspect at the end of the room. I suspect that there is an airing cupboard on the left so this space could have been used and afforded a much more spacious outlook.

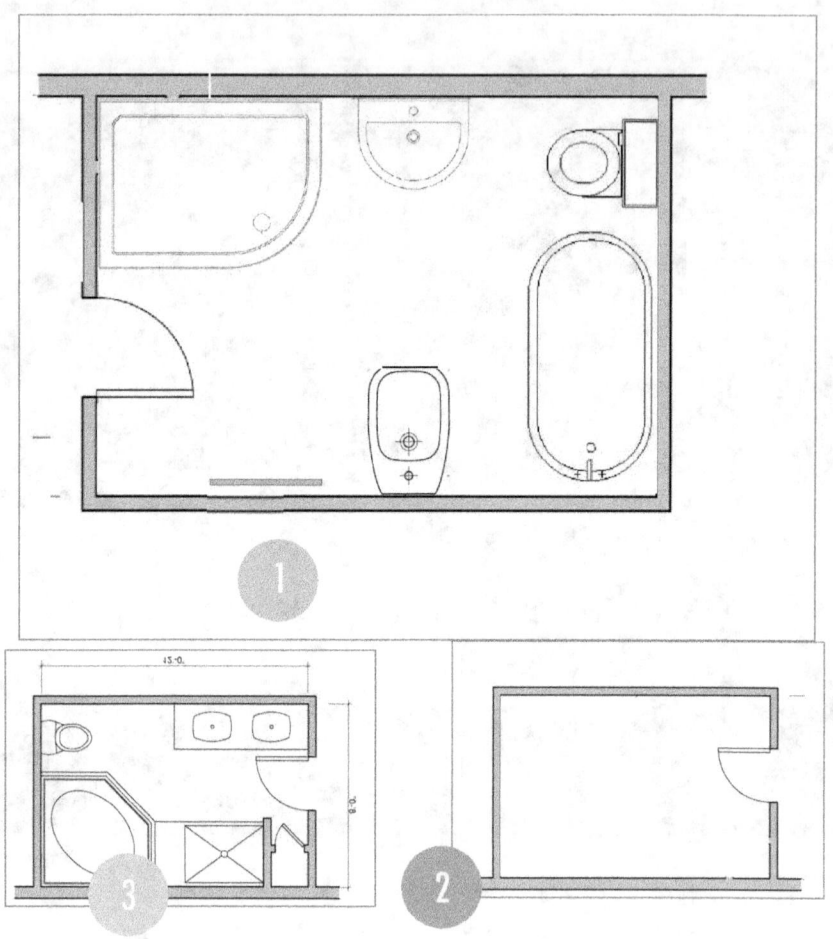

Plan 3 is the original bathroom layout before remodelling.
Plan 2 is the bathroom with the airing cupboard removed.
Plan 1 is the new remodelled bathroom.

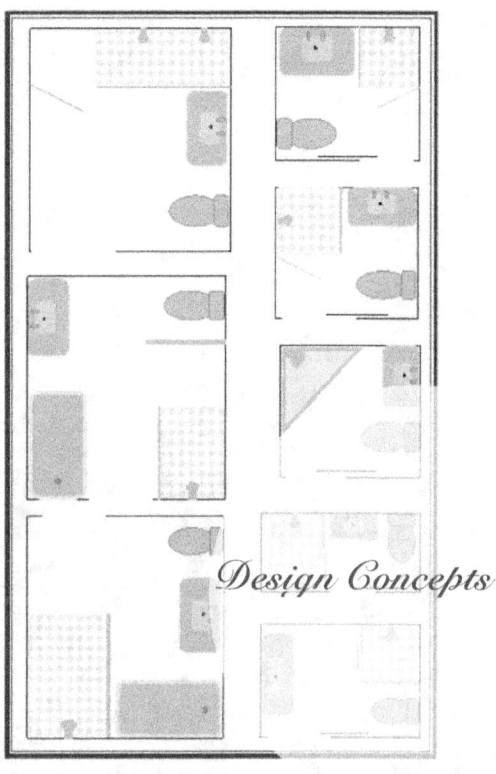

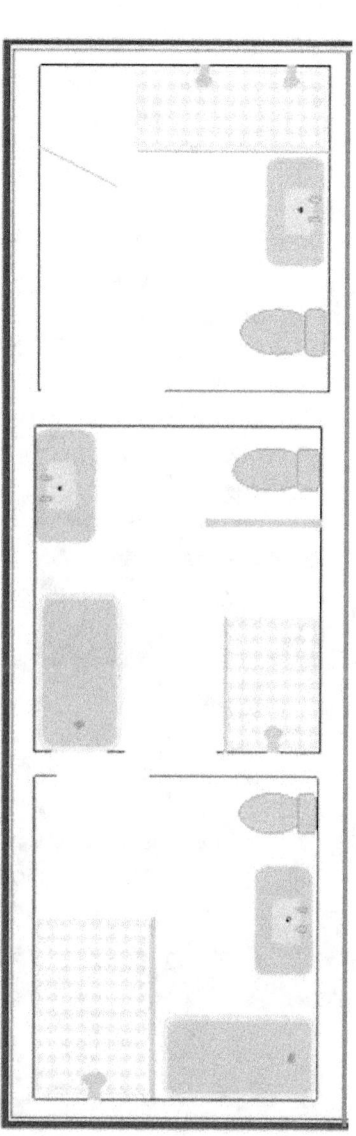

Design Concepts

TURNING A PLAN
INTO A DESIGN

All these plans are good workmanlike plans and worthy of any new home development but if the buyer has a good budget they can all be turned into designer layouts. Looking specifically at the right hand group of plans

TOP - simple vanity unit, w.c and 1200 x 760 shower. But this example has no bath so for impact I think we should introduce a bath. the position of the door is not clear. There is a door shown but this presumably is an airing cupboard so the gap at the bottom of the plan is clearly the entrance door. Ideally would be inclined to centralise the door as shown in the middle plan. In all cases I would introduce a wall hung w.c. and possibly a grouped vanity and wall hung w.c.. So we are going to open the room and incorporate the airing cupboard. According to the buyer preferences the best presentation would be to use a corner or offset corner bath where the airing cupboard is shown and a quadrant enclosure on the right hand side. in place of the existing shower. Using the combo vanity where the basin and w.c. are shown. this leaves plenty of space for radiator on the left hand side plus the possibility of his and hers vanity units with a smaller unit for him on the left hand just as you enter the room. Result a completely different view which can be accessories in any style you wish.

Middle layout

We can assume here that the buyer has a penchant for a w.c. with a modesty panel but again use the wall hung and a low level modesty panel in special toughened etched glass to taste. Bath is clearly not shown to scale so we will put that in the top left hand corner and again recommend an offset corner or small corner bath. We will introduce a his and hers double vanity to the left of the door and for space we will recommend an offset quadrant in place of the existing shower.

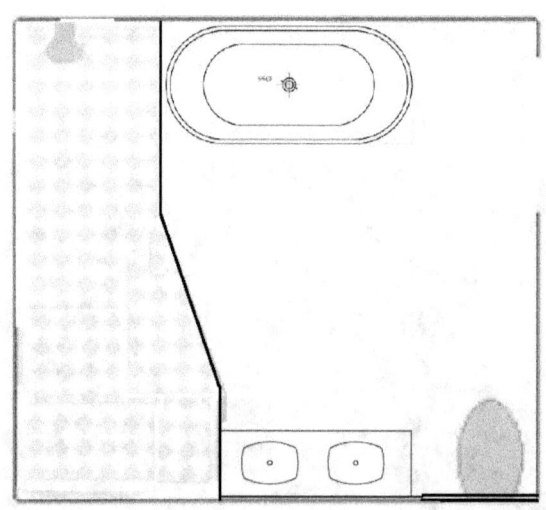

BOTTOM LAYOUT

Same size room but door position is reversed. The two square shower and bath items look very boxy so we need to rethink this area completely. clearly the door is set to one side allowing a very large wall where the w.c. is. So let's centralise the door if possible and use a trad bath set in the middle of the left hand wall. with a special semi wet room shower at the very end which will be set directly beside the freestanding bath and open out to a larger area at the bottom right hand side. There will be composite trays to incorporate a small rectangular tray and a pentangle tray but flushed to the floor. There would also be the option for steam and a steam dome. I would also recommend body jets at the wide side of the shower and a deluge head at the narrow end. We will again use our wall hung package and a his and hers basin.

See new layout above

This bathroom is a clean, modern design with some imaginative lighting Interestingly it includes a bidet and semi wall hung w.c. and that still quite rare item -the Urinoire. As usual the continent has embraced the bidet for many years and quite recently the Urinoire which avoids peeing on the floor in the middle of the night. Worth a thought. The only criticism is the mirror lighting and not using a fully fledged wall hung set.

This study is very dramatic but it is all for show and less practicality. Older people have trouble enough getting in and out of the bath without climbing through a window. Lighting around the mirror is pathetic. Why place a towel rack right in the traffic area in the doorway? The lighting is not very user friendly.

This bathroom is much nearer the mark but the lighting is dated and frankly dreadful. Most housewives these days are fastidious in their cleaning habits, especially in the bathroom. My wife would be horrified. Nice his and hers vanity but where is the bidet? The bath is a little lost in this setting. Ideally is would be best on a plinth to set it off. The vanity units are just a little too large. Rescaling these or combining would be a big help.

Too often design gets mixed up with planning. In a bathroom the only usual element of design is the finishing touches or perhaps the lighting or maybe the final decor. Design enters the equation when you are developing an entirely new bathroom and using an existing room not currently used as a bathroom where your imagination and that of the buyer can meld to produce some really interesting results, subject to the budget. Often the design element can be produced without a huge budget.

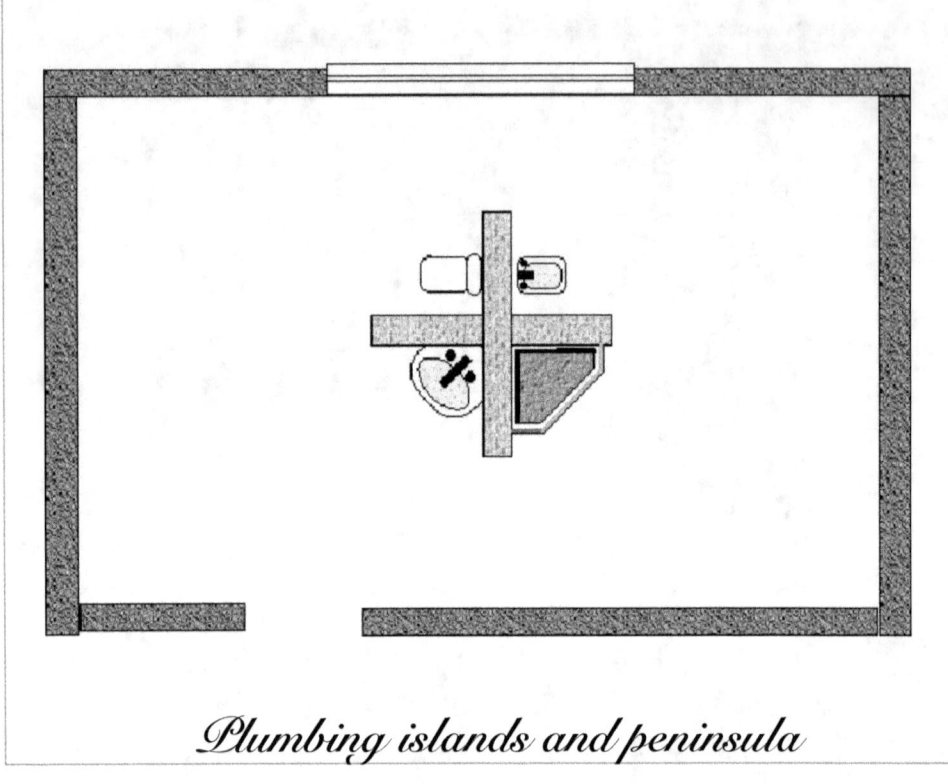

Plumbing islands and peninsula

We all know that we can box in even a 100mm waste pipe along the edge of the room generally to and from an svp but we can extend this concept to island and peninsular plumbing plans. The island above shows a fully conposite island with w.c., bidet, basin and even a shower. this is an incredibly useful concept especially when converting a largish bedroom to a full featured bathroom.

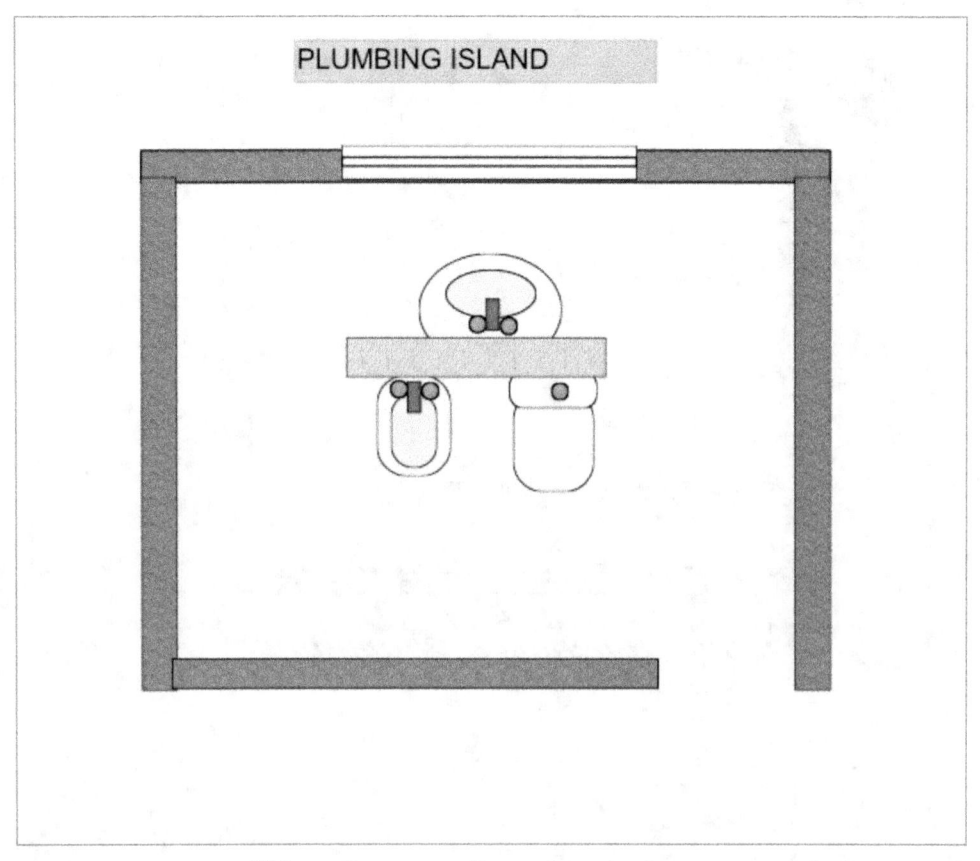

Plumbing islands and peninsula

This island is showing a w.c. bidet and basin but this sort of configuration could be expanded to even include a good size bath, especially a large spa bath or even one of the big Steam Spa bath/shower combinations.

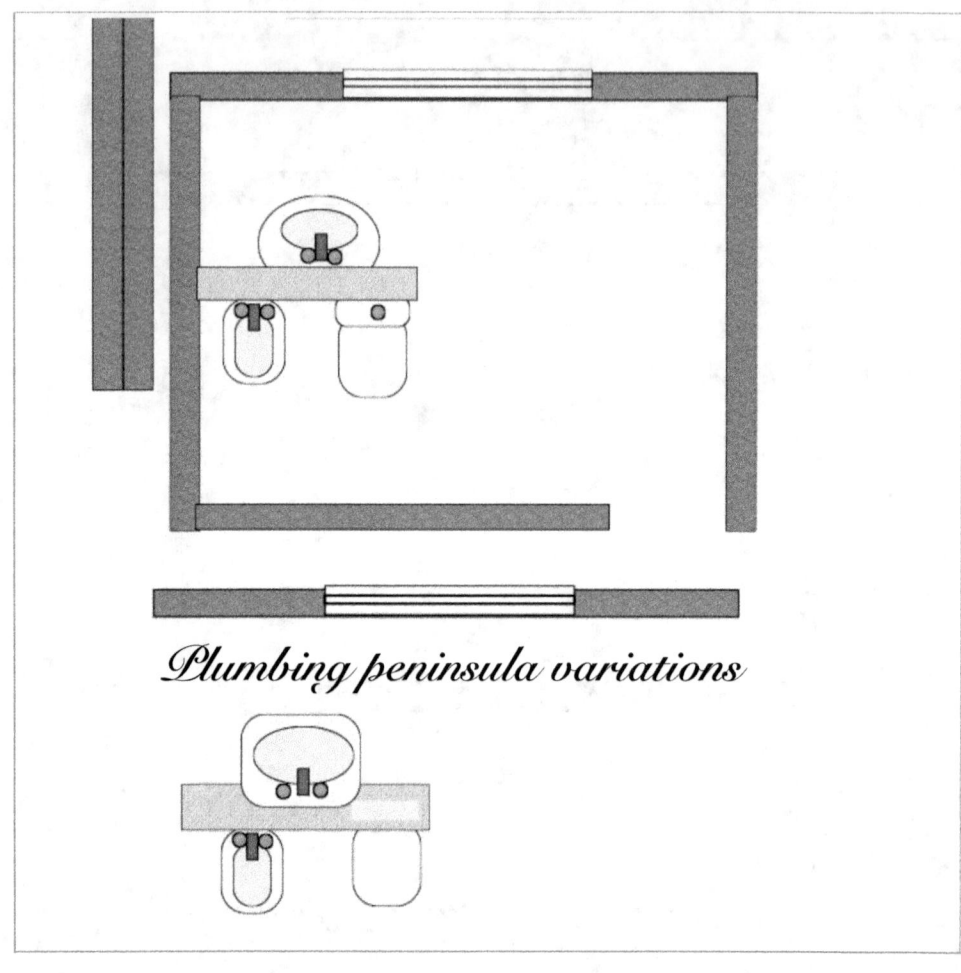

Plumbing peninsula variations

This is a study that could be used in smaller rooms, to great advantage. The upper example shows a simple peninsular possibly even branching into the edge boxing as discussed earlier. The lower example shows a slightly chunkier peninsular incorporating the concealed cistern for a btw or wall hung combi.

FINAL DECOR

* *what is the theme is the decor true to the theme*
* *is the customer staying in the property - how long*
* *don't make the final decor too outrageous or overly personal they may want to sell the scheme in the future*
* *is the decor in keeping with the rest of the property - does it complement the property or detract from it a.*

The final decor obviously depends upon the style of bathroom chosen together with the buyer and what the buyer's personal taste dictates. It is always worth pointing out, however, that if the design is too outlandish and the customer wishes to move at some time in the future you need to choose a theme which can be sold to a third party.

White sanitaryware with strong colour contrast

This is an excellent theme and one which doesn't really hit the budget too hard. In many cases the supporting/contrasting colour is just paint or at most probably tiles but it could, of course also be granite, marble or solid surface material costing £1000's

Other examples of white and colour.

these are perhaps a little O.T.T.?

LIGHTING

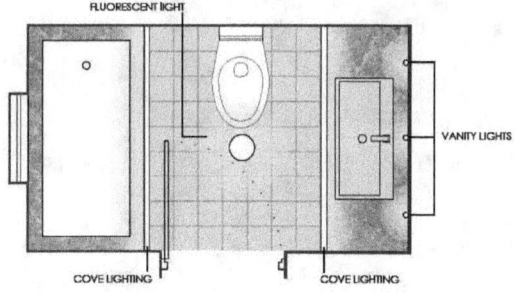

FLUORESCENT LIGHT

VANITY LIGHTS

COVE LIGHTING

COVE LIGHTING

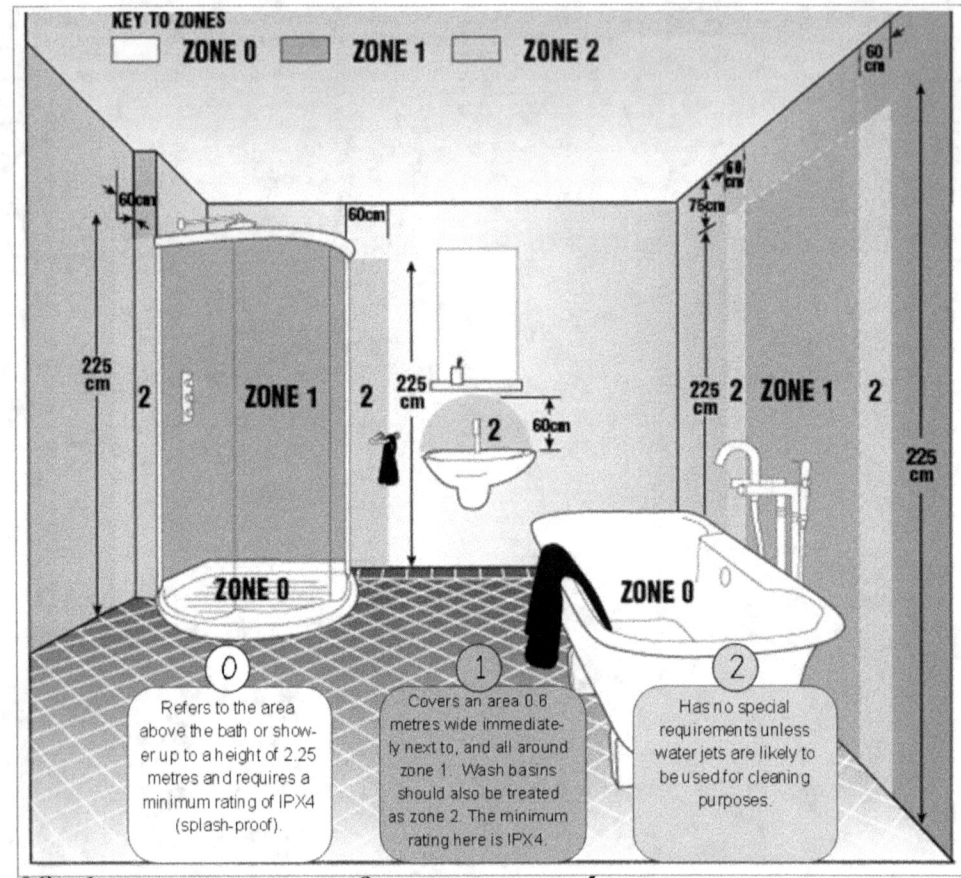

KEY TO ZONES

ZONE 0   ZONE 1   ZONE 2

60 cm

60cm

60cm

60 cm

75cm

225 cm

225 cm

225 cm

225 cm

225 cm

2   ZONE 1   2

2   ZONE 1   2

60cm

ZONE 0

ZONE 0

0 — Refers to the area above the bath or shower up to a height of 2.25 metres and requires a minimum rating of IPX4 (splash-proof).

1 — Covers an area 0.6 metres wide immediately next to, and all around zone 1. Wash basins should also be treated as zone 2. The minimum rating here is IPX4.

2 — Has no special requirements unless water jets are likely to be used for cleaning purposes.

Lighting must conform to regulations

The current IEE electrical regulations are very complex and perhaps a little confusing at times but if you study them in detail you should be able to grasp the essentials of the ideas. It is all about safety. You will also need to be aware of the IP ratings for the products which are not always well specified. remember, a good lighting budget for a quality bathroom could actually run into £1000's . Plan and sell wisely.

Bathroom Zone 0

Zone 0 is inside the bath or the shower tray itself. If lighting is required in there, any fitting used must use a low voltage supply, that is a maximum of 12v **and** also be rated at least **IPx7** which means it is totally immersion proof.

Bathroom Zone 1

Zone 1 is the area above the bath or shower tray to a height of 2.25m from the floor. Any fitting used in this zone must have a minimum rating of **IPx4*** , which means it is protected against water spray from all directions. If the fitting uses a 240v supply, a 30ma residual current device (RCD) **must** also be used to protect the circuit in this zone.

Bathroom Zone 2

Zone 2 is an area stretching 0.6m outside the perimeter of the bath and to a height of 2.25m from the floor. In this zone again an IP rating of at least **IPx4*** is required. It is **good practice** to regard the area around a wash basin, within a 60cm radius of any tap as **zone 2.**

Bathroom Zone 3 (Outside Zones)

Zone 3 is anywhere outside zones 0,1 and 2 (subject to specific limits) and where no water jet is likely to be used. No IP rating* is required in these areas.

*If there is any likelihood of water jets ever being used for cleaning purpose in **Zones 1,2 and Outside Zones,** fittings rated a minimum **IPx5** must be used which tells you that the fitting is protected against water jets.

The latest edition of the IEE wiring Regulations will provide more detailed information but your electrician should be fully up to date with these. When it comes to selecting the actual fittings to go into the different bathroom zones there are plenty to choose from.

BATHROOM REGS

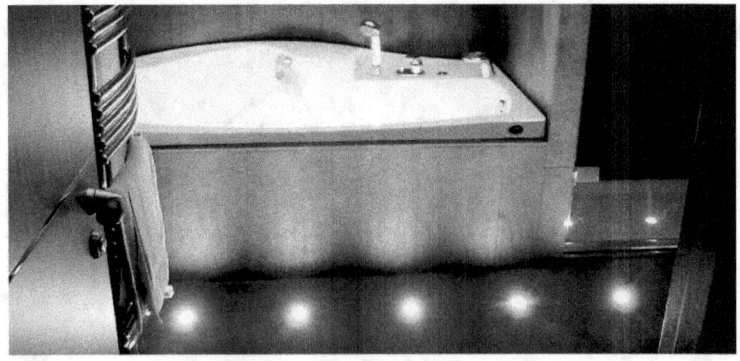

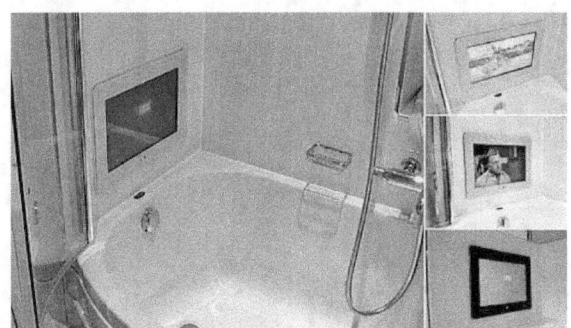

Bathroom TV - now affordable

BATHROOM TV

NOW AFFORDABLE

Waterproof Bathroom TVs

| TV In The Bath | Watch The Soaps In Peace | Reliable And Safe |

What a perfect combination, a hot bubble bath and your favourite soaps or film on the television. We stock a large choice of waterproof bathroom TVs, including styles that double up as mirrors to give that sleek bathroom look but instantly turn into a TV once switched on and styles that can be fitted into the wall for a more bespoke touch.

  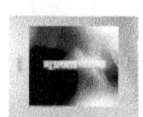

Luxurite - Waterproof LCD Television - Crystal Black Frame - Various Size...

Luxurite - Waterproof LCD Television - Silver Mirror Frame - Various Size...

26" Advanced Waterproof Bathroom TV

£658.94

£706.94

£939.95

22" Advanced Waterproof Bathroom TV

19" Advanced Waterproof Bathroom TV

19" Classic Waterproof Bathroom TV

£689.95

£479.95

£439.94

34

HIS AND HERS

One of the big trends during our Bathroom retailing operation was the growth of His n Hers Basins. This can be used in virtually any basin mode and is a sure fired seller.

His and Hers suits any theme

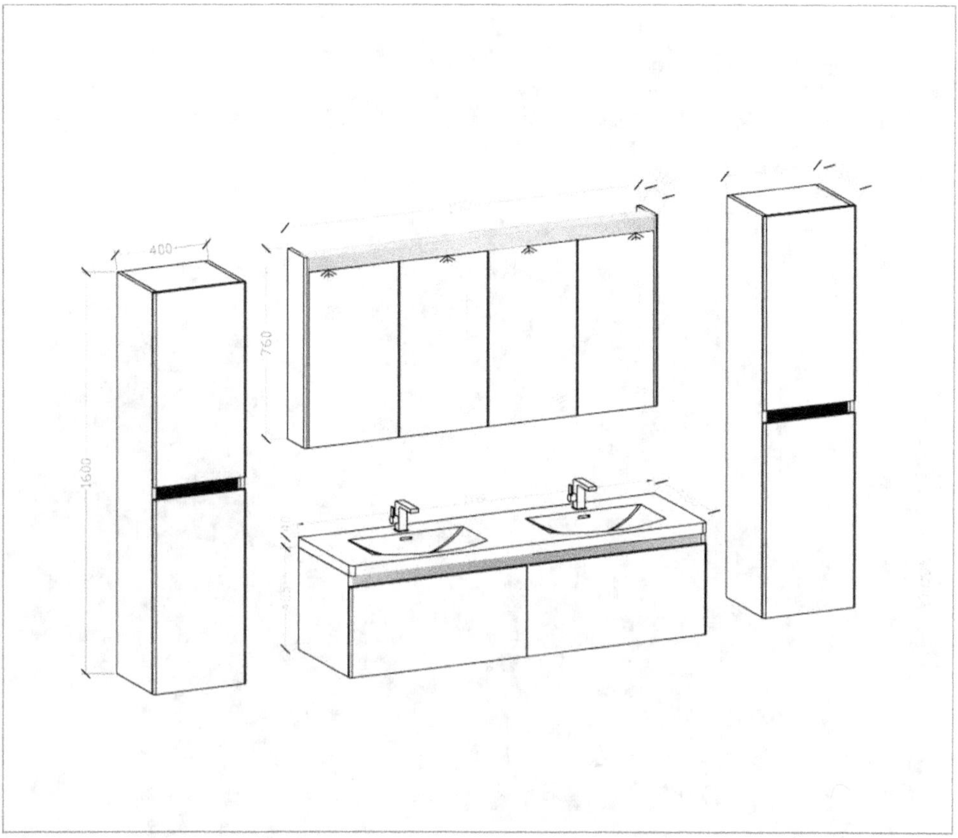

400

760

1600

Modern Wall hung or traditional

DISABLED BATHROOMS

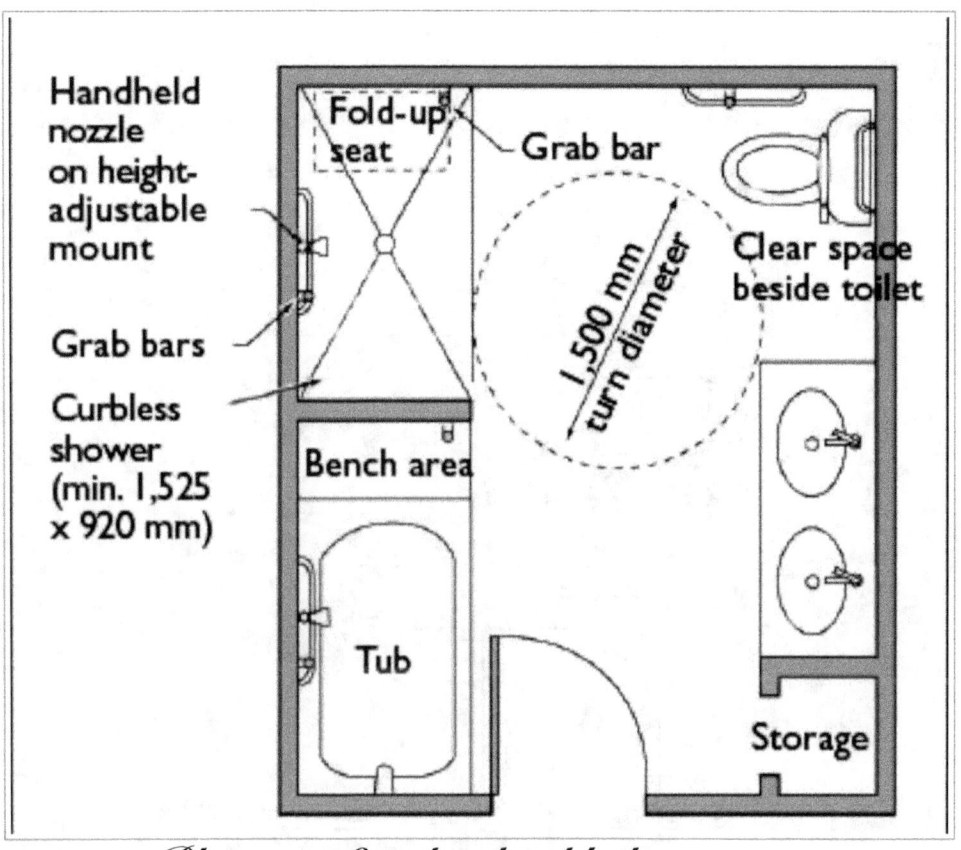

Handheld nozzle on height-adjustable mount

Fold-up seat

Grab bar

Clear space beside toilet

Grab bars

Curbless shower (min. 1,525 x 920 mm)

Bench area

1,500 mm turn diameter

Tub

Storage

Planning for the disabled

We looked at ergonomics and anthropometrics and of course this applies to a bathroom as much as a kitchen. This thinking applies greatly to the w.c. which may need to be higher and to the basin which may need to have wheelchair space. the grab bars and folding rails are also specified in the DocM disabled document and you may wish to include more around the bath or showers. There are a number of walk in baths but they are expensive and short lived. The best option is a walk in shower possibly in the form of a wet room.

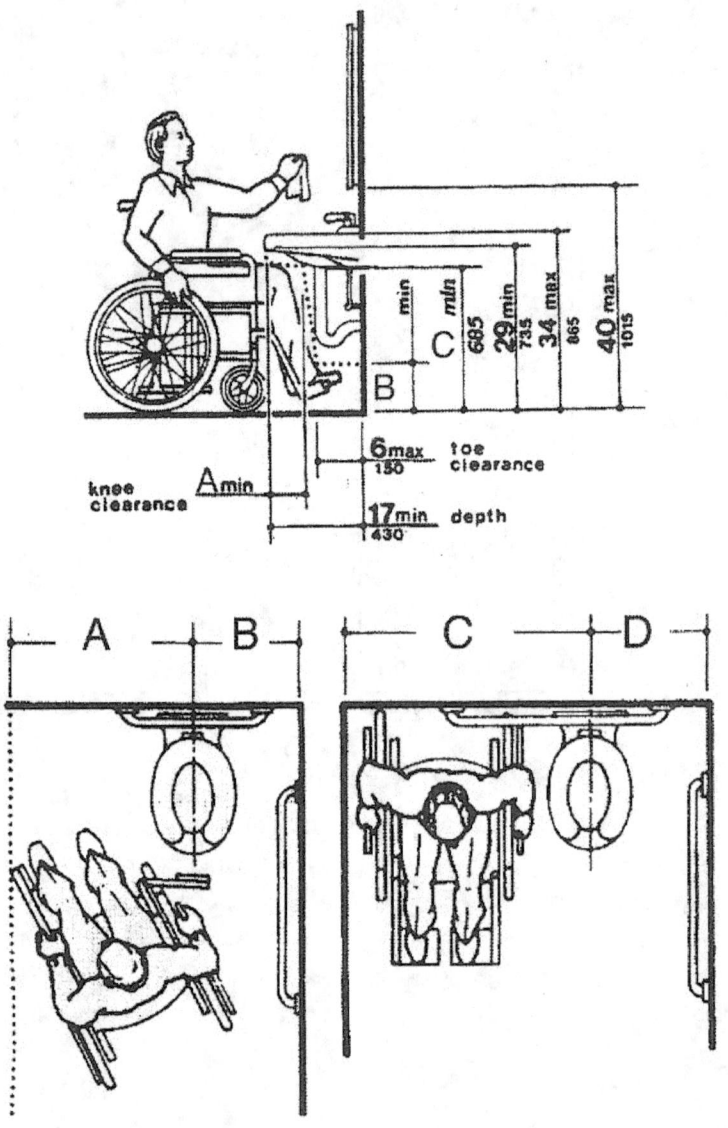

min

C min

665

29 min
735

34 max
865

40 max
1015

B

6 max
150

toe
clearance

knee
clearance

A min

17 min
430

depth

A | B | C | D

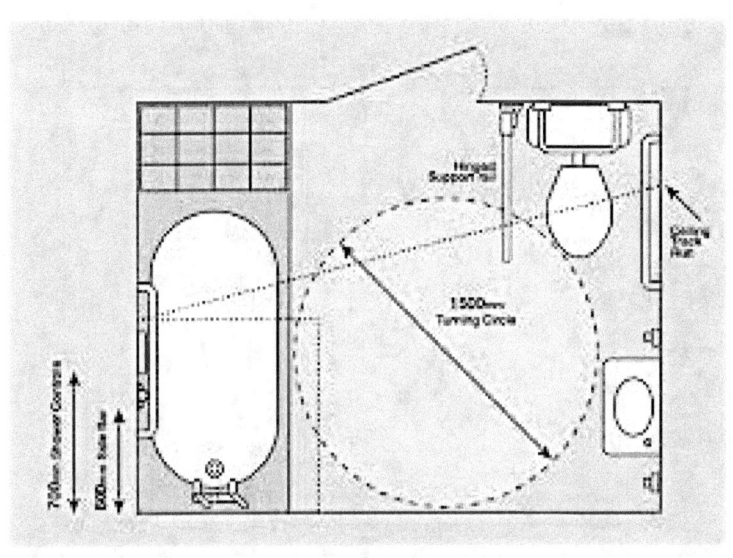

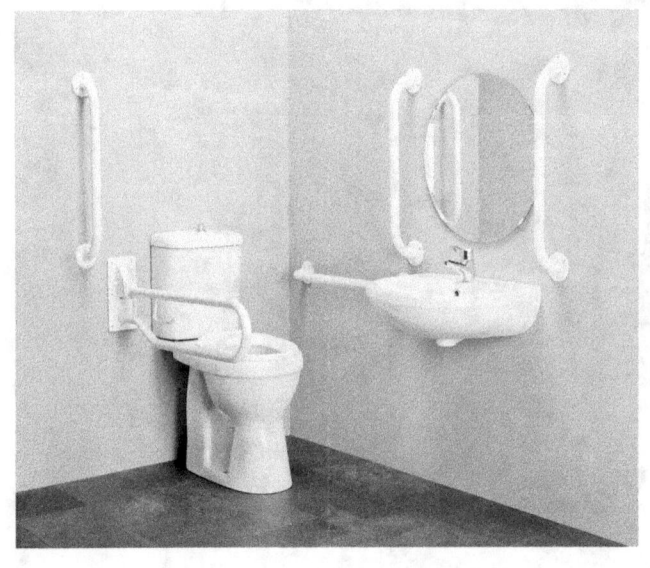

Luxury Items

Luxury items include spa baths, steam showers and the like. These items are also sold in low grade Chinese imports such as Steam Baths and composite steam devices. In our experience the life of these items is fairly short so any design should reflect the necessity of replacing these items as little as 2-3 years down the road. Always remember that steam especially requires ventilation and many of these have the ability to vent to atmosphere but in any case there MUST be ventilation in the room.

Thank you for purchasing this latest version of our 2016 mini guides. The Bathroom Designer guide is the latest of the designer guides which have only been touched on in previous full sized guides. For the first time you have enough material to progress fully into an AKBB PROF Designer qualification.

We want you to enjoy this publication and learn from it,

To this end we offer TOTAL SUPPORT - if you feel you need help or clarification on any points please log in to our website at

www.kbb2000.com

SURVEYING
TECHNIQUES

EXTERIOR
PRESENTATIONS

GRANNY
FLATS

CLOAK ROOMS
DRESSING ROOMS
CLOSETS

KITCHEN
WORKING
TRIANGLE 2016

*DOUBLE
WORKING
TRIANGLE*

CREATIVE
INTERIOR DESIGN
USING A
COMPUTER

CAD VS BRAIN

KITCHEN
PLANNING
ESSENTIALS

I POINT
PERSPECTIVE
& VANISHING
POINT

KITCHEN
PLANNING
APPLIANCES
ESSENTIALS

2 POINT
PERSPECTIVE
& VANISHING
POINT

KITCHEN
PLANING +
DESIGN

BIRDS EYE
PERSPECTIVE

BATHROOM
PLANNING

BEDROOM
PRESENTATION

BATHROOM
DESIGN

BATHROOM
PRESENTATION